Nebraska

BY M. J. YORK

The Child's World

Published by The Child's World®
1980 Lookout Drive • Mankato, MN 56003-1705
800-599-READ • www.childsworld.com

ACKNOWLEDGMENTS
The Child's World®: Mary Berendes, Publishing Director
The Design Lab: Design and production
Red Line Editorial: Editorial direction

PHOTO CREDITS: Weldon Schloneger/Shutterstock Images, cover, 1, 3; Matt Kania/Map Hero, Inc., 4, 5; Kamila Žárská/iStockphoto, 7; Shutterstock Images, 9; iStockphoto, 10, 13; Weldon Schloneger/iStockphoto, 11; North Wind Picture Archives/Photolibrary, 15; Nati Harnik/AP Images, 17; AP Images, 19; Intraclique LLC/Shutterstock Images, 21; One Mile Up, 22; Quarter-dollar coin image from the United States Mint, 22

LIBRARY OF CONGRESS CATALOGING-IN-PUBLICATION DATA
York, M. J., 1983-
  Nebraska / by M.J. York.
      p. cm.
  Includes bibliographical references and index.
  ISBN 978-1-60253-471-1 (library bound : alk. paper)
  1. Nebraska—Juvenile literature. I. Title.

F666.3.Y69 2010
978.2—dc22

                    2010017929

Printed in the United States of America in Mankato, Minnesota.
July 2010
F11538

On the cover:
Chimney Rock
can be seen from
miles away.

CONTENTS

Geography

Let's explore Nebraska! Nebraska is in the middle of the United States. This area is often called the Great **Plains**.

SOUTH DAKOTA

MINNESOTA

WYOMING

IOWA

• Chadron

Agate Fossil
Beds National
Monument

• Alliance

Scottsbluff

Chimney Rock
National Historic Site

NEBRASKA

Wayne •

• Norfolk

Platte River

Missouri River

North Platte

Grand Island

Omaha •

Bellevue

Kearney

★ **Lincoln**

McCook

MISSOURI

COLORADO

KANSAS

NORTH

WEST   EAST

SOUTH

Cities

Lincoln is the capital of Nebraska. Omaha is the largest city in the state. Bellevue and Grand Island are other well-known cities.

Nebraska is the only state that has a one-house legislature. Every other state has a two-house legislature.

More than 400,000 people live in Omaha. ▶

Land

Much of Nebraska is wide, open plains. But some of these areas are hilly. The Platte River cuts across the state. The Missouri River is the eastern border.

Nebraska has soil that is good for farming. ▶

Plants and Animals

Nebraska's state bird is the western meadowlark. The brown and yellow bird has a beautiful song. Nebraska has few trees, but it has many grasses. The state grass is the little bluestem. The goldenrod is the state flower.

Goldenrod grows wild in fields and along roads. ▶

People and Work

Nearly 1.8 million people live in Nebraska. Nebraska is known for farming. Farmers in the state grow a lot of corn. Nebraska is called "the Cornhusker State." Cattle are raised here, too. Many people work packing meat.

Corn is Nebraska's biggest crop. ▶

History

Native Americans have lived in the Nebraska area for thousands of years. The United States bought the land from France in 1803. Soon, settlers in wagons traveled through Nebraska. They followed the Oregon Trail to the West Coast. Settlers came to stay in Nebraska in the 1850s. They fought with the Native Americans who already lived there. Nebraska became the thirty-seventh state on March 1, 1867.

Settlers traveled through Nebraska in covered wagons. ▶

15

Ways of Life

Sports are **popular** in Nebraska. College baseball **championship** games are played here. A **rodeo** championship is held here, too.

The Nebraska State Fair is a popular event. It is held in Lincoln at the end of each summer.

College football is very popular in Nebraska. ▶

Famous People

Gerald Ford was born in Nebraska. He was the thirty-eighth president of the United States. Actor Henry Fonda was born and grew up in Nebraska. Writer Willa Cather lived in Nebraska. She wrote stories about the state.

Willa Cather was a famous author who lived in and wrote about Nebraska. ▶

Famous Places

Chimney Rock is in western Nebraska. It is on the Oregon Trail. Chimney Rock is 325 feet (99 m) tall from base to tip. Nebraska is a good place to find **fossils**. People learn about fossils at Agate Fossil Beds National **Monument**.

Chimney Rock has been a National Historic Site since 1956. ▶

21

State Symbols

Seal

The Nebraska state seal shows the state's rivers, farms, and hills. A cabin with crops stands for farming. Go to childsworld.com/links for a link to Nebraska's state Web site, where you can get a firsthand look at the state seal.

Flag

Nebraska's state flag was adopted in 1963. The state **motto** is "Equality Before the Law."

Quarter

Chimney Rock is on Nebraska's state quarter. The quarter came out in 2006.

Glossary

championship (CHAM-pee-un-ship): A championship is the game or series in a sport that is played to decide the winner of the year or season. Nebraska hosts a baseball championship.

fossils (FOSS-ulz): Fossils are the remains of animals or plants that lived millions of years ago. Nebraska has many fossils.

legislature (LEJ-iss-lay-chur): A legislature is the group of people who make laws for a state or country. Nebraska has a one-house legislature.

monument (MON-yuh-munt): A monument is an object that honors a person or an event. Agate Fossil Beds National Monument is in Nebraska.

motto (MOT-oh): A motto is a sentence that states what people stand for or believe. Nebraska's state motto is "Equality Before the Law."

plains (PLAYNZ): Plains are areas of flat land that do not have many trees. Nebraska has plains.

popular (POP-yuh-lur): To be popular is to be enjoyed by many people. The Nebraska State Fair is a popular event.

rodeo (ROH-dee-oh): A rodeo is a contest in which people ride horses and rope cattle. Nebraska holds a rodeo championship.

seal (SEEL): A seal is a symbol a state uses for government business. Nebraska's state seal shows the state's nature and farms.

symbols (SIM-bulz): Symbols are pictures or things that stand for something else. Symbols for the state are on Nebraska's seal and flag.

Further Information

Books

Keller, Laurie. *The Scrambled States of America*. New York: Henry Holt, 2002.

Shepherd, Rajean Luebs. *C is for Cornhusker: A Nebraska Alphabet*. Chelsea, MI: Sleeping Bear Press, 2004.

Zollman, Pam. *Nebraska*. New York: Children's Press, 2007.

Web Sites

Visit our Web site for links about Nebraska: *childsworld.com/links*

Note to Parents, Teachers, and Librarians: We routinely verify our Web links to make sure they are safe and active sites. So encourage your readers to check them out!

Index